IN YA FACE

Rik George

In ya face contacts: rikspoems@googlemail.com

ISBN 978-1-4452-1358-3
90000

Regarding poetry,

why not be frank, say it as it is, call a spade 'a spade'...

That way, there is no confusion.

Clarity, is sanity.

R.

CONTENTS

IN YA FACE

In ya face.
Ya know
so close
their breath hits ya cheek.
Imposed spatial sharing nullifies need for booming voice -
instead
macro zoom captures precisioned pitch
but with fever
so ya spit   a little.

No wasted word
no beatin bush
forget florid, cryptic decoration;
trash ambiguous, saccharine-stained sentiment; cus
lethal overdose on unequivocal
musters plain, simple
bladed cuts.

DIDDLY SQUAT

diddlysquat.com
whatyagot.com?
notalot.co.uk

lost all me money
playin' online poker
notveryfunny.com

at first I was
www.winning
dreaming of beaches
in faraway places
those beautiful girls
with such beautifulfaces.com

mother said I was
www.sinning
it'll all go wrong
you markmywords.co.uk

bollocks to that
forward slash
don't be so daft
I know what I'm doing
dot com

it was all looking great
www.letscelebrate!
full house
kings over tens
such a great hand
oh come to me girls
on the sun drenched sand

thought it was mine
a huge pot of wanda
payoffmeloan@phew
forward slash
in debt nolonga

I just couldn't believe it
couldn't Adam 'n Eve it as
it all went wrong
www.sadsong
when full house
kings over jacks
was shown

BUGGER IT!
mumwozright
@confessions
forward slash
backward
step dot
com

only last week

I was swimmin' along fine

livin' life to the full

sat steady in the saddle

now I'm near drownin'

livin' life lousy

up the bloody swanee

without a bloody paddle

diddlysquat.com

whatyagot.com?

notalot.co.uk

MANIKIN

Manikin manikin
give me your hand
and let us go dancing on shining white sand

Manikin manikin
lend me an ear
so whispered sweet nothings can show you I'm near

Manikin manikin
offer me your eyes
so we might seek lanterns in dark clouded skies

Manikin manikin
loan me your nose
so we can sniff out where the warm wind blows

Manikin manikin
tender me your shoulder
for something to cry on when the warm winds blow colder

Manikin manikin
you've been falling apart
since that day in the window when you stole my heart

INTERNATIONALLY FUNDED ROCKET LAUNCH

High five

Four sprung durch techniks

Three-wheeler Reliant Robin

Tou-louse

Juan

Lif tov!!!

CARIBBEAN WITNESS

Here
as I sit
on me doorstep
as the sunshine reaches
from the forests to the beaches
I witness before me
the tourist's adulation
f'dis precious leetle nation
dis Caribbean world of magic potion
with smiles full of sunshine
dis luscious land
of elegance, fragrance, casual style
and no such ting as a four minute mile.

What make you come all dis way?
Tobago
it's a hell of a long jurrrr-neeey
all day
in a plane
to Port of Spain
then on again.

I suppose
(though a don't really knows)
that it muss be de sun
that attract de Englishmun
as it beats
in de gardens
on de streets.

Also
I happen to know
that the Englishmun is quite ecstatic
with the lack of frantic antic
ambling through the leafy glade
with towel
sun-spec
and a bucket and spade.

Tobago
to go slow
oh yes though
the visitor can learn
from the lady
sat over dur
she takin it Eee Zee
no sense of Urr Gen Cee
just limin'
ain't no quartz precision timin' on dis island.
You worry and you hurry
sense-less-ly scamperin' around
in your far off land
don't you understand
the triviality of your relentless patterns of needless activity?
Oh why d'ya dilly dally up ya heart attack alley –
it's a serious business is dis!

"Don't know dis place called Heart Attack Alley,"
says the lady
sat over dur
with the puzzled face
"but I once knew a girl called
Haversack Sally
she got arrested
unofficial business
street queen
if ya know wat a mean
could av got away
if she'd knowed a running way. . . "

Maybe if you visit
dis delectable nation
dis delicious land
you will understand
feel the proportion
of still and motion
satisfaction
is lack of action-pack desire.

Just sit
like me
on me doorstep.
Look
learn
and perspire.

COSMETIC RHAPSODY
(aka Bohemian Surgery)

Sing:

Is this my real wife?
she's just had surgery
boob-job and face-lift
an escape from reality

Open your eyes
look down to your thighs and see
you're getting old dear
losing your dignity;
you've got a
lazy eye
bulging tum
six false teeth
saggy bum
ya mouth's so big the wind blows
(but it) doesn't really matter to me

to me

LARGE PEOPLE

N.B. Best read slowly, out loud, and with a Brummie accent.

large people
miss trains
moving around
slowly
blindly
in circles
eating burgers
drinking cola
making smiles

large people
put their feet up
on footstools
sleeping
snoring
dreaming
about their pet dog

large people
loom large
when laid out
end to end
on stage
at the annual lounge room lizards awards ceremony

large people
take the p out of pavements
stare angrily at staircases
ignore escalators
and look nervous when approaching revolving doors

large people
drive clapped-out vans
watch soaps
congregate largely in small shops
and are commonly
to be seen
passing time
in Post Office queues

large people
wear enormously out-of-shape jumpers
and baggy trousers
(which they call slacks)
and silver streaked training shoes
with luminous orange laces

large people
threaten tsunamis
making waves
belly-flopping
in hotel pools
in Torremolinos

large people
are not great on safari –
they despise sunshine
and jungle
and jeeps
and straw huts
(and Africa)
and simply hate not being one of the Big Five

large people
can be seen standing
linking arms
in October
at high tide
on harbour wall
looking out to sea
acting as hugely effective
human flood defences

large people
smile profusely
at harrowing news
of uncle Bob's
obese niece (Kylie)
tumbling off
a treadmill machine
at the local gym
in Dudley

large people
are occasionally discarded
from fishermen’s nets
mistakenly harpooned
off the west coast of Cornwall

large people
miss trains
reacting slowly
departure change
from platform 5
to platform 3
preventable life perplexity
throws brain off kilter
would rather eat burger
drink cola
make smiles

GLOBAL WARMING	***TO BE PERFORMED AS A ROUND*** PLEASE NOTE: Further groups may be added to make a more complex round (depending on the number of available lifeboats)	
Group 1	*Group 2*	*Group 3*
Global warming		
Global warming		
Fetch the engine	Global warming	
Fetch the engine	Global warming	
Fire! Fire!	Fetch the engine	Global warming
Fire! Fire!	Fetch the engine	Global warming
Pour on water	Fire! Fire!	Fetch the engine
Pour on water	Fire! Fire!	Fetch the engine
Too much water	Pour on water	Fire! Fire!
Too much water	Pour on water	Fire! Fire!
Fetch the lifeboat	Too much water	Pour on water
Fetch the lifeboat	Too much water	Pour on water
Flood! Flood!	Fetch the lifeboat	Too much water
Flood! Flood!	Fetch the lifeboat	Too much water
Stack the sandbags	Flood! Flood!	Fetch the lifeboat
Stack the sandbags	Flood! Flood!	Fetch the lifeboat
No more sandbags	Stack the sandbags	Flood! Flood!
No more sandbags	Stack the sandbags	Flood! Flood!
Fetch the army	No more sandbags	Stack the sandbags
Fetch the army	No more sandbags	Stack the sandbags
Help! Help!	Fetch the army	No more sandbags
Help! Help!	Fetch the army	No more sandbags
Like a war zone	Help! Help!	Fetch the army
Like a war zone	Help! Help!	Fetch the army
Save the ozone	Like a war zone	Help! Help!
Save the ozone	Like a war zone	Help! Help!
Politician	Save the ozone	Like a war zone
Politician	Save the ozone	Like a war zone
Why? Why?	Politician	Save the ozone
Why? Why?	Politician	Save the ozone
'Cus you ought a	Why? Why?	Politician
'Cus you ought a	Why? Why?	Politician
	'Cus you ought a	Why? Why?
	'Cus you ought a	Why? Why?
		'Cus you ought a
		'Cus you ought a

Act 1: WHEN YOU'RE NOT HERE

Like a steam train without rails
Like the sun without the moon
Like a hammer without nails
Like a song without a tune

Like Canterbury without Chaucer
Like a jack without a box
Like a cup without a saucer
Like ticks
without tocks

Like the summer when it's over
With the sun behind a cloud
Like the dog who feels forgotten
When it says no pets allowed

Like a ship without an ocean
Like a springtime without May
Like a tube of sun tan lotion
On a cold and rainy day

Like a solitary milk bottle
Toppled over on the ground
Like a chest of buried treasure
That never will be found

Like a book without a cover

Like crying without a tear

Like love without a lover

That's how I feel when you're not here

Act 2: FRICTION

inner linings

lie bruised, beneath

whilst

smiles entwining

gather sharpened teeth

as

chair reclining

lures second hand blonde

whilst

wizard whining

wields second hand wand

aboard virulent airborne virus

friction enters

alights

responds

Act 3: DIVORCE IS

Divorce is

inevitably undertaken when marriage is irretrievably broken
not very nice at all
a synonym for failure
a new beginning,
    which you can't fully appreciate until you later look back

caused by writing on the wall
hard to fully explain how it got to this
hard for those not involved to understand . . . why?
people saying (to you)

    "but you've always looked so happy together"

people saying (about you)

    "I knew it would never work"

in another stress league to moving house
a song by Dolly Parton
not very common in Italy
invariably messy, especially if there are kids
    (then it gets irretrievably and inextricably messy)

a shock for your best mate
invariably the result of shit hitting the fan instead of the pan
about losing friends and making new solicitors
about siding with one party or the other, or neither, but never both
an anagram of d'ceivor
expensive
dividing things up equally, in favour of the woman

PUNNET

Punnet.

Such a fabulous word
just say it
slow
pierce your lips, pronounce the 'p' and let it go -
'p' - unnet. . .
not loud though
cus it's cute
it's sweet
what you give
is what you get
like a pet
a pet punnet.

Pick yer own rasps
and put em in the punnet
pick em quick
pop em in
lovely
av ya dun it?

Punnet
say it
slow
pierce your lips, pronounce the 'p' and let it go -
'p' [ha]
breathy, like a whisper (so ya hear the 'h')
go on

just say it

and you'll know what I mean

it's the lemon

and the curd

such a fabulous word

'P' - unnet. . . !!

LONDON UNDERGROUND

IN!

enter station – steps – cavernous concrete reverberation – ticket machine – clunk – please take ticket – queue – wait – queue – wait – turnstiles – queue – clickity clack – through – and on – cavernous concrete reverberation – and on – step stepity steps – escalator – no choice – (no steps) – must go on – queue – down and down – darker and dark – buzzing sound – clatter – muffled – chatter – down – I'm drowning – help – help! – going under – must stay afloat – surging crowds – only way out is ahead – can't go back – but wait!

a slight dispersal – confluence of two platforms – sucking people in two directions – distant roar – getting closer – distant roar still roaring but now, not quite so distant – getting louder – newspaper headline on platform floor reads:

CAVERNOUS CONCRETE REVERBERATION SUBSUMED BY GIANT ROARING MACHINE ON RAILS –

the giant machine is slowing, it's slowing – slowing down – stop – loud fizzing sound as sliding doors fizzily slip apart – stepity step as people alight – one – after another – after – another – after – like wildebeest in flight racing across the plains – wildebeest in flight – and on – we get – and on – we get – one – after another – after another – like wildebeest swimming across the river and climbing up onto the riverbank – loud fizzing sound as the doors fizzily close - and away we go – speeding up – faster and fast – but no space – breathe – must stay – afloat – alive – squashed – shuffle – about – must try – to find space – no seat – (no space) – no air – then suddenly slowing – slower and slow – and slows – and stop – step over case – push past pram – fizzing sliding fizzy doors slip fizzily open – and out – pushing past more pushy people pushing prams – then steps – and queue – and up – and steps – and up – and queue – and clickity turnstile clack – and cavernous concrete reverberation comes back – and crowds – and pushing – and need to stay afloat – and on – and through – and light ahead – must focus on light – only way is ahead 'cus there's no way back – and on – and through – and focus on light – and on – and through – and on – and through – and up – and on – and up – and on – and up – and lighter – and light – and exit – and

OUT!

FATHER TIME

My father grew vegetables.
He took his time.
He made time
for his favourite pastime,
always showing care and precision in his timing.
He made sure
that he found the time
to show care and precision in his timing.
And timing, of course,
is everything.

My father was at one with the soil.
The soil was at one with my father.
Both made each other,
at the same time.
My father was a beautiful man.
A man of his time.

These days,
I wish more people grew vegetables.

CONDOMINIUM

If I lived in America
I'd buy a condominium
And tell my friends in Nottingham
That I lived inside a condom.

Safe.
Warm.
Protected.

I would . . .

TERRORIST TERRORIST

Terrorist Terrorist
please stop trying to blow my brains out
so you can find your heart

Terrorist Terrorist
please stop trying to cut out my tongue
so you can have your say, but I can't have mine

Terrorist Terrorist
please stop trying to gore my eyes out
so only you can see the light

Terrorist Terrorist
please stop trying to remove my legs
so you can stand where I stand

Terrorist Terrorist
please stop trying to decapitate me
so you can place your head on my shoulders

Terrorist Terrorist
please take my hand
and together we will find our soul

DONNA KEBAB AND SHIRLEY KNOTT

I once knew a girl named Donna Kebab.
Donna Kebab.
Donna Kebab, yes
Donna Kebab
with a very big nose
and a mouth so wide
that it looked like her tongue could pull you inside, and
once inside
she'd suck out your brains.

A strange little girl
she was in my class
doing O Level Maths
on the day that the world did explode.

She was sat beside a girl named Shirley Knott.
Shirley Knott.
Shirley Knott, yes
Shirley Knott
now I know it sounds crazy
but you have to believe me
it's true.

Now Donna tells Shirley
that she's got up the duff
after intimate exchanges
and licking
and prodding
and sucking
and Donald Ducking
with a boy named Fred,
Fred McGoven.

I remember quite clearly
(they were both sat quite near me)
that the class went hush
as the following words
were set down in history
(even though it was Maths).

Said Shirley,
"a bun in the oven
from freaky Fred McGoven
you've got to be joking,
surely not."
Surely not.
Shirley Knott had said,
"surely not"!!

Well the class began to laugh . . . .
and they laughed
and they laughed
and they laughed
and they laughed
and they laughed till they started to cry.
And they laughed so much
that the school closed early
for fear that someone might die.

Poor Donna
poor Shirley
an unfortunate pair
and that's not one word of a lie.

I once knew a lad named Arthur Pint.
Arthur Pint.
Arthur Pint, yes

Okay . . . .   that's a lie.

FAT

yuk!

makes me want to p-

yuke

Em **** ic

Liposuction

= totally taking the

'phat'

out

WITHOUT THE 'L'

sex, sex, sex
always on my mind
every hour, every minute
and all the secs
of every day

they call me the 'the 24 hour clock'
but without the 'L'

REGISTRATION

1. PRIVATE SCHOOL

OK class
do listen carefully
and answer your name
with the utmost clarity

Bridges

Sir

Buckley

Yes indeed Sir, present Sir

Miss Hamilton

Present

Miss Hardingham-Jones

Present

Proudlove

Sir

Richardson

Sir

Miss Sherdon-Futherton-Mott

Present Sir!

Thank you class
oh wonderful class
oh joy oh thrill
lovely boy lovely girl
what a pleasure it is to teach you

2. STATE SCHOOL

OK class
shut up and listen
just answer your name
and we'll see who's missin

Duckit

Sir

Horris

Sir

Lockit

Urgh?

Morris

Sir

Pickit

Yeh

Pickit

Yeh

Pickit!!

Sir

Smith

Sir

and Wackit

Wackit?

Eric Wackit?

Wackit's waggin it Sir
gone into town Sir
to buy some porn Sir
to get some smokes Sir

yes alright

he's waggin it Sir
he's waggin it Sir

yes alright alright
he's absent

waggin it

absent

twat

what was that?

Thank you class
oh wonderful class
what thrill
what joy
loverly girl
oh boy
what a pleasure
it is
to teach
you

waggin it

EASTER

Why is Easter
Never on time?
Why is Easter
Never on time?

Sometimes early
Sometimes late
Sometimes making
April
wait

Why is Easter
Never on time?
Why is
Easter
Never on
Time?

DEECE MORONING IN PARKY

very nasty thing
appen ed to me
whilst walking deece moroning in parky

leetle boysy
e come oop to me and sez
you speak English?
yiss I sez
e sez
i lose ed my mommy in parky
wud you elp me pleece?
of course I sez
let me take you by the handy
and we go find your mommy

so there we are
walking handy handy
and next thing i know
deece very large chav lady
woz hittening me
with big steek
she sez
give back to me my leetle Billy
you strange pervey man
I sez
stop hittening me pleece big scarey chav lady
the leetle boysy woz lost ed

but she woz aving noon of eat
and to cut a long story shorter
a policeman lady come to parky
and take ed me away for passport cheek

person ali, I dunno what is appeneding
as me only going for walk in parky
person ali, I dunno what deece country is combing to. . .

TRAILER

On cold pavement slab she lay
motionless,
twisted shape.

Two puncture wounds to the neck;
a bite?

Slow trickle of thickening blood seeking the valley between
her naked breasts.

Her eyes! Oh my God, look at her eyes!
The horror, sheer terror in those eyes!

God alone knows the limits of her suffering. . . .

' Traffic Warden 2 '

At a cinema near you

from Sunday.

LIFE

menstruation
impregnation
jubilation
education
graduation
vocation
remuneration
vacation
consolidation
medication
cessation
incarceration
salvation
infestation
that'll be life then
sianara
Amen

15. reincarnation?

ASHES TO ASHES

To commemorate 01 July 2007

Dearly Beloved
We are gathered here today
To celebrate and mulleth over
The invasive life of the cigarette smoker
The troubles and the strifes
Of the gasper and the choker.

We are gathered here today
To coiffeur obscenities and blissfully ridicule
This perpetual creator
Of joyful song unsung
Of browning teeth and rotting lung
Of stench
Of sorrowful faces
But who
From this day forward
Will violate my precious air space no more
In enclosed public places.

We are gathered here today
To commit his ashes
To a continent of death, remembering
Those stale malodorous odours of his
Foul repulsive breath, to
Say one last good-bye
To the vicious evil sod

Whose fate

Itself

Is now

To die.

Ashes to ashes.

Dust to dust. Thank God.

ICKERS

frilly knickers

eyelash flickers

alan's wickers

city slickers

potato pickers

tocking tickers

magic trickers

cocky dickers

hiccupping hickers

roneo vickers

right-click clickers

lollipop lickers

a parrot

sick as

GAME, SET AND MATCH

now correct me if I'm wrong

(15 - Love)

but the basic premise

re: the art of playing tennis

is

the ability

the facility

to run about

whilst holding a racket

so to get to the ball

and wack it

yes?

(30 - Love)

so when this geezer

(last Sunday, down the park, in a wheelchair, no legs, one arm, name of Haggerty, invalidity, what a pity)

(30 – 15)

so when this geezer

comes up to me and says

fancy a game a tennis mate?

forgive me for thinkin

that this guy

must be blinkin

bananas

(40 – 15)

okay so far? got the picture?

I mean

what would be the point?

one could hardly delight in

thrashing him
takin advantage of the poor man's plight
able bodied athlete verses wheelchair Pete
just couldn't be right
delicate affiliation meets potentially loaded situation

(40 – 30)

so I ducked out saying
so sorry mate
got to go and cook the dinner
or the wife'll go ballistic
cast a spell
cast me out
supercalifragilistic
know what I mean?
pathetic excuse

(Deuce)

no worries
he replied
I'll find someone else

(Advantage Haggerty)

and he did
and I watched
while he played
a competitive game
of competitive tennis
with a man named Stan
who knew no prejudice
and I felt sad
with myself

and that is the story
of my incorrect presumption
my complete lack of gumption
last Sunday
down the park

(Game, Set and Match Mr Haggerty)

FREE-FALL

i'm all of a

p'panic

cus i'm fall-ing, free-f'

falling

unopened chute

my para-

chute! (catchabreath,

catcha

catch it, now s'su   ck

it in)

i plummit

to earth

quick as a wooosh

                life's flicked film

                                rolling

break-

                                neck

                lick before me

                                                flailing kicks

                                useless

(fail-ing)

oh no!

oooooooooooooooooooooooooo

ooo0ooo0ooh

shi-

(THUD)

it

•

JIM NASTIC

(for Georgie)

On the floor
he went hands in the air, pause   and then
tumble tum bletum ble tum ble
tum-ble-tum-ble-tum-ble spot.

On the beam
he went backward flip, heart stops   and then
totter t'totter b'balance don't f'fall!

On the vault
he went   spring   and   through   the
  air   and   thud.

On the Pommel Horse
he went tuckty fluperty tuck tyflup with neat   lyneat   ly
tuckty fluperty tuck tyflup with neat   lyneat   ly he went
tuckty fluperty tuck tyflup and neat ly off and stop and phew!

On the rings
he pull ed   himself   u   p
into a   spl   it s   position.

On the bar

he went roundandroundandroundandround

like one

profound

stuck-record sound

          stuck-record sound

                    stuck-record sound

My mate Jim,

Jim Nastic.

NIGHT OUT

1. Monica (aged 16 today) is sat with her forehead, lead weight, resting on a corner table. She is completely rat-arsed.
2. Alan has had 4 pints of Stella and 4 vodka shots.
3. Sarah, his girl, has had 9 white wine spritzers.
4. Johnny has started to get aggressive which is what happens when he drinks too many triple rum n' cokes.
5. Ian has had 7 pints of Stella.
6. Beryl, has had 7 pints of Stella.
7. Stella (the person) doesn't exist, which is a shame for the writer.
8. Beryl doesn't fancy Ian, which is a shame for Ian
9. Col has had 4 pints of real ale (he is taking it easy as he is driving).
10. Avril is throwing up outside.
11. Anthony, is asking Avril, his girl, to hurry up so he can get to the bar (he is one pint behind Ian and has got a real thirst on).
12. Sue is Col's girl. Sue can't take her drink. Sue has drunk 'a lot' of drink. She has got a real thirst on but can't find the bar. This is unsurprising.
13. Big Ron is drinking cider. No one is clear on how much Big Ron has drunk.
14. Everyone is clear on why Big Ron is called, 'Big Ron'.
15. Graham, the glass collector, is hurriedly collecting glasses. His progress is suddenly hampered when for no apparent reason, he is threatened by
16. Johnny.
17. Elaine has had 18 vodka shots. She has gone to the ladies with Janet so to gossip about Col, cus she saw him with that slut Babs Dumpleton earlier this afternoon and he's almost certainly up to his old cheating tricks again, and that would explain why he was late,

screwin' around, just like he did when Elaine was his girl, the two-timin'

18. bastard.

19. Poor Sue.

Has anyone seen Sue?

20. Happy birthday Monica.

ENGLANDO!

Lampardo
Gerrardo
Rooninho
GOOOOOOOOOOOOOOOOOAL!!
One nilo!
Beautiful gameio
Jogo bonito
Just like Brazilio
All end in O ya know
Just like Jairzinho

Englando!
Feel the passion and the soul
Curving ball io
On the grass io
It's Crouchio
With a
Headio
GOOOOOOOOOOOOOOOOOAL!!
Two nilo!!
Beautiful gameio
Jogo bonito
Just like Brazilio
All end in O ya know
Just like Ronaldinho

Then I woke up

Englando?

Just like Brazilio?

Don’t be stupido!!

Dream onio . . . . .

England 4 Moldova 2

Some people are on the pitch. . . .

They think it’s Moldova. . . .

It is now!!

WHEN BLACKBIRDS SING

When blackbirds sing
and raindrops tap and then

bounce

off my window panes
and a leafed page flickers when occasionally turned
and I'm all curled up like paper when it's burned
and my duvet cover's ruffled and pulled up high
up to the tip of my chin
on a Sunday morn
in the middle of May

then all is calm
and calm is lovely
and lovely is best
like the inside of a flower

and another world
in another place
with its worlds of woes
with its faster pace
is for now
at least

forgotten

BREAST

I was sat next to a girl
just the other day
on the number seven bus
she was going my way

She was cuddling her baby
when it started to cry
I was reading my paper
when I started to sigh

"Excuse me," she said
"but it's time for his feed"
didn't grasp what she meant
I continued to read

Now I have to be frank
the girl was very well endowed
with a priceless pair of knockers
of which I'm sure she must be proud

So when she loosened her bra strap
and released a massive tit
it took up so much acreage
that I moved along a bit

Even though I felt embarrassed
I couldn't bring myself to quibble
as the mother held her breast out
and the baby grabbed her nipple

Though I'm still not sure it's decent
people claim it's naturale
for some mums, accepted practice
and it isn't illégale

All I know is I was shaken
from this so publique display
but you'd best hear my confession
that it rather made my day!

PIANO

My piano
is my oldest, bestest friend.
Depending on my mood
I can caress it
or I can bash it
I can molest it
or I can completely and insanely thrash it
as it succumbs
in masochistic splendour
to my intrusive fingering technique.

It responds by saying
            more
            give me more
in audible moans of
rapturous, chromatically shifting harmonic surrender.

Thank you friend
forever faithful
always there
upright, in the corner

waiting

NEWY ORK

. . . but it's just a piece of modern art Officer Ziegler,

abstract expressionism, rando-

m construct,

pulsing canvas

of strings and skeins of enamelled

grain, some matte, some glossy, weaving/running an intricate web of tans, blues, greys,

lashed through with black and white sssssss-

patters.

It's just a piece of modern art Officer Ziegler, see?

> *From the artist:*
>
> "Dazzled by neon, nobody knows/cares where they go or how they get there, moving in tangential direction is pre-requisite, so you criss-cross over peoples' lives, toes, reflections."

Don't you get it, Officer Ziegler? 20 deep on sidewalk/pavement go the

paintbrush lines, drip

style, show harsh, thick, curve, raised, only occasionally fine tip. Look! See

that Giant Taxi, dis-

carded blob of yellow streak heading north on Madison,

ain't so easy cus one-way equals no-way out onto fifth, henceforth the artist's

wrist arcs/flicks new avenue slipping

east past the Rockefeller, makin' sure the taxi don't

knockafella over or even off the canvas altogetha, as

car

eats car

eats car/man

eats skyscraper

eats waffle

eats Japanese woman tourist posing for photo with big bronze sculpture of a bull whose rampaging horns and enormous Jackson Pollocks add a neurological numbness to the texture off battery park (see, there in the top left hand corner)

it's the New Apple

it's the Big Yorkie

Newy Ork it's

just a piece of modern art Officer Ziegler

just m O dern,

a Ziegler piece of it's

arT

Officer

just abs-

tract ex pressio ni sm,

ran-do m

construct

see?

GERBIL

one gerbil
rat
two gerbils
ratatooi
three gerbils carrying Kalashnikov rifles
rat a tat tat
four gerbils in business suits
pro ratas
five gerbil tight-rope walkers
vermin on the ridiculous

. . . OF JURY SERVICE

When in court
on Jury Service
used to sit
next to this
very young girl
had no brain
quite insane.
How on earth
can recent birth
limited life experience
neuro interference
rightfully convict   or
rightfully acquit
man on charge
counter espionage
stuff about spies?
Difficult decision
for anyone with vision
never bloody mind
when you ain't got a clue
if what he said was true
or a pack of lies.
Complex case
ifs and buts
wherefores and whys
eleven angry men
and a silly little girl -
a plank in disguise.

Fortunate twist
too much doubt
judge intervened
case thrown out!

For thine is the kingdom
the power
and the jury
for ever and ever
Amen.

'THE JOYS'

. . . OF TEACHING (aka 'The Art of Fart')

when in class

with turbulent arse

used to stand

next to kids

sat at desks

and let one go

creeping evil

SBD*

horse and cart

and then return

to teacher base

front of class

and watch

and listen

to accusation

without foundation

as someone else

is blamed

for making

smells

silent, **but deadly*

STAFF ROOM SKIES

picture the scene
crowded staff room
morning break
lots of chatter
bout kids
and teaching
and holidays
especially the latter

picture the scene
around my table
four or five teachers
supping tea
partial escape
temporary refuge
from life in the trenches

picture the scene
assumed normality
away from the bunker
me
the regular, dedicated biscuit dunker
my perfect theorem
of weight x heat x time
respected and admired
by teachers far and wide

picture the scene
considered calm
no need for the napalm
as dunking my digestive
no eyebrow was raised
no eyelid batted
as I held my biscuit
a split second too long
in the very hot liquid
picture the scene
developing irregularities
impending hostilities
the challenge laid down:
could I snatch the sagging suggestive
deliver the drooping digestive to my mouth
before the dunk
was sunk
in my tea?

picture the scene
as like a lizard's tongue to a passing fly
I retrieved the falling, billowing bomb
with such talent and dexterity
with such deft refined biscuitry
with professional aplomb

and then someone laughed. . . .

weight x heat x time stood still
reciprocal laughter I couldn't resist
as my mouth burst open
the biscuit exploded
and life ceased to exist

picture the scene (now in slow-mo)
a mushroom cloud of atomised biscuit particles
shattered
and then consumed the staff room skies
colleagues ducking
then leaping for cover
oh the screams and the howls
oh the shrieks and the cries

yes, picture the scene
reputation in tatters
no chance for reprieve
only one way forward
a sharp exit
a shameful retreat
so off I went.
Absent WithOut Leave. . .

12 ½ %

<u>Oh we do hope you enjoy</u>

<u>your meal with us!</u>

But don't forget to read the small print

or you'll sure get a **BIG** surprise!

service charge applies:

12 ½ %

cheeky bastards

LIFE BREATH

breathe in de rhythm of de reggae reggae beat
syncopated sounds suck a shuffle from ya feet
listen to de bass low frequency vibration
listen to de life breath of a Caribbean nation

it goes
doon chaga
doon chaga
in und out

doon chaga
doon chaga
in und out - it goes
doon chaga
doon chaga
in und out

and den it gets
inside ya head

ya see
de rhythm   go in

but it never fully   come out

man

IGNORANT COW

Good morning
I said
to the lady on reception
on my very first day at work.
Perhaps she didn't hear me
for her reply was not returning
no tricks intended
no catch
no deception
just a chance
to snatch
an early hour discourse
to prepare a way
at start of day.

Good morning
I said
to the lady on reception
on my very second day at work
and just a little louder than before.
Perhaps she didn't hear me
for her response was not forthcoming
surely
my passing act of courtesy was inviting
not cost incurring
simply civil
being friendly
just natural decorum
re: reception area forum.

Good morning
I said
to the lady on reception
on my very third day at work
and just a little louder, little louder than before.
No tricks intended
no catch
no pretension.
No reply.
No reciprocal attention.
No nothing.

Nowt.

Now give me credit
for my persistence
but I hope I'll never
need to seek assistance
from this
IGNORANT
COW!!

LIFE, AT THE CREM

Life
at the crematorium
is perpetual death ad nauseam
perpetual death ad nauseam
perpetual death ad nauseam.

At 4.13
my auntie
who had no breath left
leapt off the conveyor belt of life
and was rolled ontothe conveyor belt of death.
Just the regular Crem service you understand
sing a hymn
close the curtains
wheel the next one in.

Now there's something quite cold
about these once in a deathtime occasions.
At 93
this life was surely deserving of warmer celebration.
Half-way through
whilst my heart was sinking
the vicar eyed his wrist-watch
4.22
what time's the next one due?
I heard him thinking.

Maybe it has
to be
like this
a life for a life
need to make room for the next one I guess

cus more is less
so best get em sent down quick!
Abide with me
better miss out verse three
cus Mrs Patterson's due at 4.34
ooops time is pressing
only one minute left for the boiled down blessing.

At service end
we are ushered outside
to the backyard of the living
to briefly admire
such warm coloured flowers
for today's Crem dead
an almost pitiful
(but beautiful)
abundance of flora
saliently set on cold concrete slabs.

'For Edna'
'For Ernie'
'Uncle Harold'
and
'For Sam and for Dora'
Now where have they put my poor auntie's flowers?

Ooops I almost forgot
to thank the vicar
for the beautiful service. But where's he gone?

Of course. . .

It's 4.34
and poor Mrs Patterson's a knockin' at the door.

Life
at the crematorium
is perpetual death ad nauseam
perpetual death ad nauseam
perpetual death ad nauseam.

SHERBUT FOUNTAIN

FIRST

ya bite da end off da hollared out lickriss stick
den ya suck up da sherbut
and it tastes real fab

dus

suck suck suck
up da lovely dust
delicious nectar
sweet tangy powder
suck suck suck it up
suck suck suck
and den
and den

da hollared out lickriss stick gets blocked up
and dat's really dispointin

tis

SECOND

ya BLOW!!
ya blow down da hollared out lickriss stick
hard . . .
MISTAKE!!
cus boooof!
da fountain explodes
(probly ow it gets it's name)

and a cloud a sherbut fills da air

dus

and it turns ya hair white
but it always appens dat way
so it's OK
and also funny

tis

TURD

da paper tube gets wet wiv spit

dus

and when it's soggy
it's not nice anymore
so ya loosen da sherbut
by squidgin da paper tube
and ya tip it back in ya mouth
den ya eat da lickriss
but da sherbut
is da best bit

tis

BALLY BALL

I know
let's invent a new sport
that only the Brits play
and noboby else knows nowt about
and let's call it

I know!
Let's call it

Bally Ball!

and let's get so dam good at it
that in 2010
we apply for Olympic Sports Status
and get it
and then be the only team
to enter a team
and so
win GOLD
in 2012
in London
at Bally Ball
cus there's only
one medal
anyway

COOL GUY

Roger.

One
very
cool
guy
salsa
dancer
smooth
romancer
slick
dresser
sharp
answer
but

Roger had a stutter.

Occasional nerves
a slight heart flutter
caused inde   cision
con fusion
s'stumble
c'clutter
in is ed
found it hard
to get his words   out
to speak
to utter
n'nothing

n'nowt

came out

just couldn't

get past

the word that was

last

did it matter?

Not to Rog;

met life

full in face

never one to dwell

to duck

to dive

to dodge.

One day

the coolest guy I've ever known

calls me up on the telephone

"Hello Rik it's Ro - Ro - Ro - hello

Rik it's Ro -

Ro Ro - hello, hello Rik it's -

it's Ro - Ro - Ro. . . . "

So what would *you* do?

Intervene?
Help him out of potentially embarrassing scene?
Or pretend nothing's wrong
and let him per
sist
respect his quest
to endure
to attempt to complete
his awkward little song.
Rightly or wrongly
I helped him along
and set him free:

> "Hello Roger, how are you?"
> "Hello Rik"
> said Roger
> "How'd ya know it was me?!"

No doubt in my mind
a cast iron bet
the coolest
guy
that I ever
m'met

BREATH

love evry thin about you gal
you sexy little minx
love evry fin about you gill
except your breath
it stinks

of fish

UPON HEARING THE WORDS OF STEPHEN HAWKING

Upon hearing the words of Stephen Hawking
one can't be unimpressed with his bold circumspection
his luminous hypotheses of
calculated wisdom
wrapped in synthesized speech.

How perfectly in focus
are his statements so plain
not blinding us with science
no self interest in self gain;
just a bubbling need
to present a troubling thought
to tell us all
that man
may
some day
destroy himself.
Fact.
An unstoppable force
almost certain to happen
and probably soon.

We should buy a second home
on Mars
or on the moon
cus although time and space
have no beginning
have no end

this is unlikely to be the case
for our totally screwed up, deluded human race.

Once we're broken
we will not mend
cus all things being equal
there'll be no corrective sequel
No Human Race 2
No twistin' again (like we did last summer)
No Jesus to reprise us.

So hold tight world
cus this guy knows his stuff.
A synthesized
vocalized
survivor of the species.
And Hawking's
talking
tough.

CYCLISTS

Just one or two lines about cyclists
It's not that there's so much to say
'Cept keep disregardin' the red light
Flashin' blues will be comin' your way

You think that you know so much better
When there's always more misses than hits
But your arrogant 'stuff the law' attitude
For ever will get on my tits

INTERNET AUCTION

VERY VERY RARE AND COLLECTABLE ! ! !

The following are available as a job lot

All in immaculate condition

1 quiet road for Sunday only driving
A set of old fashioned values (c.1930)
A smile that costs nothing

A pair of whistling lips

1 British person's national identity
A policeman when you need one
2 hours of quality time
A pair of pumps (child size 4)
Some respect for authority

1 chance romantic meeting on a train
(like in 'Brief Encounter')
A roll of Izal toilet paper (still in wrapper)
Another pair of whistling lips

A farmer (complete with tractor) who actually pulls over
to let you through on a busy main road
The name 'Ernest'
An inviting log fire for when it's snowed

BID NOW - Offers in excess of what is realistic!!!

Watch this item - in My Distant Memory

ITTER

banana fritter

facebook twitter

horror film jitter

bosoming titter

shagpile fitter

pathetic little quitter

annoying little shitter

arf a pint a bitter

Eartha's kitter

school yard litter

polar-neck knitter

bread

pitta

FOR WHEN YOU NEED PRETTY WORDS

The following have been collected over a number of years. I hope you enjoy them.

<u>Please note:</u> If only one word per line, count to 3 before moving on to the next word/line. If more than one word per line, a 1 second gap between words will be nice/pretty.

cup

trinket

succulent apricot

sprinkle dalliance thyme

lush green

chime

sanguine

truffle petal lace

graceful translucent shape

twinkle!

chime

plethora

reminisce, merengue, velouté, flambé,

(a little) hush, shhhhhh

shhh. . .

cu p

www.ingramcontent.com/pod-product-compliance
Ingram Content Group UK Ltd.
Pitfield, Milton Keynes, MK11 3LW, UK
UKHW041925190726
13854UKWH00003B/1459

9 781445 213583